Uncharted, Unexplored, and Unexplained

Scientific Advancements of the 19th Century

Antoine Lavoisier
Father of Modern Chemistry

Mitchell Lane
PUBLISHERS

P.O. Box
Hockessi

Uncharted, Unexplored, and Unexplained

Scientific Advancements of the 19th Century

Titles in the Series

Visit us on the web: www.mitchelllane.com
Comments? email us: mitchelllane@mitchelllane.com

Uncharted, Unexplored, and Unexplained

Scientific Advancements of the 19th Century

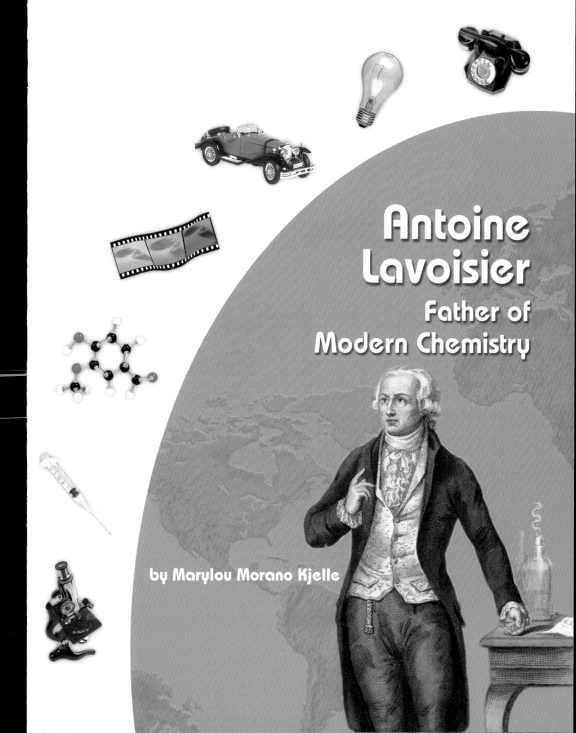

Antoine Lavoisier
Father of Modern Chemistry

by Marylou Morano Kjelle

Uncharted, Unexplored, and Unexplained

Scientific Advancements of the 19th Century

Mitchell Lane
PUBLISHERS

Printing   1   2   3   4   5   6   7   8
    Library of Congress Cataloging-in-Publication Data
Kjelle, Marylou Morano.
    Antoine Lavoisier : father of modern chemistry / by Marylou Morano Kjelle.
        p. cm. — (Uncharted, unexplored, and unexplained)
    Includes bibliographical references and index.
    ISBN 1-58415-309-1 (lib. bdg.)
    1. Lavoisier, Antoine Laurent, 1743–1794—Juvenile literature. 2. Chemists—France—Biography. I. Title. II. Uncharted, unexplored & unexplained.
QD22.L4K54 2005
540'.92—dc22

                                                                                                                    2004009310

ABOUT THE AUTHOR: Marylou Morano Kjelle is a freelance writer and photojournalist who lives and works in central New Jersey. She is a regular contributor to several local newspaper and online publications. Marylou writes a column for the *Westfield Leader/Times of Scotch Plains—Fanwood* called "Children's Book Nook," where she reviews children's books. She has written ten nonfiction books for young readers and has an M.S. degree in Science from Rutgers University.

PHOTO CREDITS: Cover, pp. 1, 3, 12, 18, 21, 26, 28, 34—SCETI Collection/Edgar Fahs Smith Collection; p. 6—Paris Digest; pp. 8, 10—Corbis; pp. 9, 15—insecula.com; pp. 30, 40—University of St. Andrews; p. 36—The Metropolitan Museum of Art, New York; p. 41—History of Science.

PUBLISHER'S NOTE: This story is based on the author's extensive research, which she believes to be accurate. Documentation of such research is contained on page 47.

The internet sites referenced herein were active as of the publication date. Due to the fleeting nature of some web sites, we cannot guarantee they will all be active when you are reading this book.

Uncharted, Unexplored, and Unexplained

Scientific Advancements of the 19th Century

Antoine Lavoisier
Father of Modern Chemistry

*For Your Information

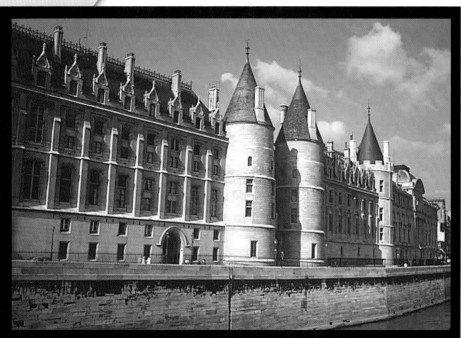

Antoine Lavoisier and thousands of others arrested by the Revolutionary Tribunal during the French Revolution were confined in the Parisian prison, the Conciergerie, while they awaited their fate. Most were beheaded by the guillotine.

1

An Accused Criminal

Torches lit the way as a procession of four covered wagons rumbled through the streets of Paris. It was the evening of May 5, 1794, and a group of men was being transferred to the dismal prison known as the Conciergerie. There they would await trial before the Revolutionary Tribunal, a special court set up after the French Revolution to try those suspected of plotting against the new republic of France. One of the prisoners was Antoine-Laurent Lavoisier.

The fifty-year-old Lavoisier was prepared to answer the tribunal's charges. He was not a criminal, he was a scientist known throughout all of Europe and in America as well. His ideas and experiments had changed the way scientists viewed the world and what it is made of. Lavoisier had taken ancient theories and transformed them into an exact science called chemistry. He had designed a way to name chemicals so that chemists everywhere could speak the same language. Lavoisier liked to think he had caused his own revolution. He called the changes he had made a "revolution in chemistry and physics."

Lavoisier had done important work outside the laboratory also. He had used his knowledge of science to help people grow better crops. He had worked for fairer distribution of tax payments, and had encouraged the government to educate children. He had designed a way for farmers to have an income in their old age. He had studied prisons and hospitals and suggested reforms. He had improved and increased gunpowder production, making France a stronger nation.

These accomplishments did not matter to the leaders of France's new government, the National Convention. For hundreds of years, France had been ruled by royalty who lived lavishly while the poor went hungry. The king and queen supported their extravagant lifestyle by taxing the people. They also used the tax money to fight the Seven Years' War in Europe and the Revolutionary War in America. By the mid 1780s, there was no money left in the French treasury.

King Louis XVI was just 20 years old when he was crowned king of France in 1774. He was a poor ruler who often took the advice of his wife, Marie Antoinette, over that of his experienced ministers.

When King Louis XVI (1754–1793) demanded more tax money from the people, they rebelled. The French system of tax collection was an unequal one. The aristocracy paid little or no taxes, while the lower classes were heavily taxed. Now the lower classes refused to be taxed further. On July 14, 1789, an angry throng of people took over the Bastille, a fortress in Paris. Poor farmers and peasants attacked members of the aristocracy in their country homes. The French Revolution had begun.

By 1792, a lawyer named Maximilien-François Robespierre (1758–1794) emerged as France's new leader, and France was declared a republic. Robespierre had many ideas about how to change the country. One of them was to do away with anything and anyone that had ties to the monarchy. As France's political and social situation fell apart, the country was caught in Robespierre's Reign of Terror and its mock justice system, the Revolutionary Tribunal. An appearance before the tribunal almost always resulted in the death sentence, with execution by guillotine. Even the monarchy was not spared: In 1793, King Louis XVI and his wife, Marie Antoinette, were beheaded.

As Lavoisier prepared to go before the tribunal, he knew that all of the good he had done for France and the rest of the world would be outweighed by one thing. Long before the monarchy had been overthrown, he had been part-owner of a company that collected taxes for the king. Lavoisier had performed his job with honesty, and had even worked to make the tax laws more equal. Others were not so honest. Many cheated the people by demanding more tax money than was necessary. Others collected taxes and did not turn them over to the government. In an effort to purge France of everything associated with the old government, all the tax collectors had been arrested and their property seized. Now, as they arrived at the Conciergerie, these tax collectors knew that soon they would be on trial for their lives.

Maximilien-François Robespierre was a lawyer who came to power during the French Revolution. He is the leader most associated with the "Reign of Terror," and was executed in 1799.

Once at the Conciergerie, the men were registered and locked in prison cells. It was a bitterly cold night, and there were few blankets and even fewer beds. Two nights later, as his cell mates slept fitfully on the floor or on hard wooden benches, Lavoisier remained awake, writing to his cousin, Augez de Villers. "I am writing today," the letter said, "because tomorrow I may not be allowed to do so. . . ."[1]

King Louis XVI was declared a traitor to the people of France by the National Convention and executed on January 21, 1793.

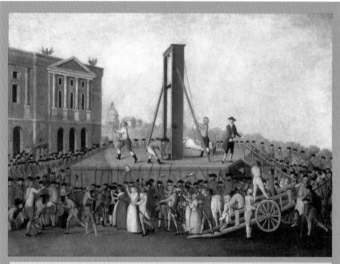

The common people of France resented the extravagant lifestyle of Marie Antoinette. She was beheaded on October 16, 1793.

Charles Dickens was a writer whose poverty-stricken background inspired him to write many books about the oppressed and downtrodden.

A Tale of Two Cities *is a fictionalized account of the French Revolution. It was first published as a series in 1859, nearly sixty years after the revolution had ended. Master storyteller Charles Dickens (1812–1870) wrote* A Tale of Two Cities *from the point of view of the commoners and peasants turned revolutionists. One of his reasons for taking the side of the "lower class" may have come from his own background. Dickens was raised in poverty in the slums of London, England. This made it easy for him to identify with those who were downtrodden and oppressed. Dickens used this viewpoint in many of his novels.*

Before the French Revolution, the common people of France had no democratic freedoms. A Tale of Two Cities *reveals the violence that results from years of oppressive tyranny. In Dickens's own country,* A Tale of Two Cities *threatened the aristocracy. The British rulers felt that by writing about oppression in France, Dickens was also calling attention to the social conditions in England, such as labor and education, that needed to be addressed.*

When writing A Tale of Two Cities, *Dickens referred to Thomas Carlyle's book,* The French Revolution, *for historical accuracy. After it was published, Dickens was criticized for not presenting a more balanced view of the French Revolution. Today students study* A Tale of Two Cities *for both its literary and historical merit.*

Sidney Carton is one of the main characters from Charles Dickens' book, A Tale of Two Cities

Antoine Lavoisier often collaborated with other scientists. Here he is in his lab with one of the four "French Chemists," Count Claude-Louis Berthollet.

2

Ambitious Antoine

Antoine-Laurent Lavoisier was born in Paris on August 26, 1743, to a family that had prospered from trade and from working for the French monarchy. In the 1500s, one of Antoine's ancestors, also named Antoine, had been a horseman for the king. Antoine's father, Jean-Antoine, had been born in Villers-Cotterêts, a small country town fifty miles northeast of Paris. He came to Paris, the "cultural capital of Europe," to study law. Jean-Antoine was guided in his career by his uncle, Jacques Waroquier. Waroquier was a member of the *Parlement de Paris*, the highest court under the French monarchy.

In 1742, Jean-Antoine married Emilie Punctis, also from Paris. Emilie's family had made their fortune in the meat industry. Her father, Clement Punctis, was also a member of the *Parlement de Paris*. He was a barrister, a lawyer who represented people in court. The Lavoisiers belonged to the bourgeoisie, the French middle class. Not as wealthy as the aristocracy, they lived comfortably and were considered well-to-do.

Antoine was the first child and only son born to Jean-Antoine and Emilie. Two years later, his sister, Marie Marguerite Emilie, was born. Antoine's mother died soon after Marie's birth. Jean-Antoine then moved his family into Emilie's mother's home on the rue du Four-Saint-Eustache in Paris. There Antoine and Marie were looked after lovingly by their grandmother and their mother's younger sister, Constance, who taught the children their lessons. Vacations were spent in Villers-Cotterêts on the family estate.

Antoine was fair-skinned with chestnut-colored hair and brown eyes. He was intelligent and serious, yet timid. When the boy was eleven years old, Jean-Antoine enrolled his son in the private school that he had attended, the School of the Four Nations. The school was also known as the Collège Mazarin after the Roman Catholic Cardinal who had once been an adviser to Louis XIII. At Collège Mazarin, Antoine studied science, mathematics, history, and literature. He also showed an interest in writing, theater, and speech-making, and in 1760 he received a prize for composition. One of his professors, the Abbé Nicolas Louis de La Caille, recognized Antoine's talent in science and taught him the importance of exact calculation and logistical reasoning. These two principles would later help Antoine bring about his "chemical revolution."

In June 1761, Antoine left the Collège Mazarin, but without a bachelor's degree. To please his father, he entered the Paris School of Law. Marie had died at the age of fifteen, and it fell to Antoine to fulfill all of his family's ambitions. Father and son were very close, and Antoine did not want to let his father down. Inside, however, he yearned to study science, to learn the "movements of the atmosphere."[1]

During the summer of 1763, Antoine traveled France's Valois region with his father's friend, a well-known geologist named Jean-Étienne Guettard (1715–1786). From Guettard, Antoine learned about mineralogy and geology. The following September, Antoine began taking the examinations for the bachelor of law degree. Even while studying law, he did not abandon his interest in science. In his spare time, he studied mineralogy, botany, and anatomy and physiology. He was also interested in the relatively new field of electricity. His first scientific paper was on the aurora borealis (northern lights). He claimed they reminded him of "the folds . . . and shadows of a white drapery."[2]

Whenever Antoine studied, he was able to concentrate so hard nothing would distract him. Studying became his entire life. He rarely went out because he felt more comfortable alone in a laboratory or library than with other people. The young scientist stopped eating regular meals and drank only milk so that he would have more time to study.

Lavoisier attended lectures at the Jardin du Roi (the Garden of the King) given by the well-known chemist Guillaume François Rouelle (1703–1770). Lavoisier was very ambitious and at first tried to study all the sciences at once. Later, he concentrated on geology and mineralogy. Still later, he began

In Lavoisier's time, the Jardin du Roi (Garden of the King) was a center for scientific learning. Today an aquarium, a zoo, and several museums are located at the site.

studying chemistry, the science of matter. He knew that a good foundation in chemistry would help him understand mineralogy.

Mid-eighteenth-century chemistry was very different from the chemistry we know today. Then, scientists were just beginning to explore the elements that make up the world. Before this time, they had relied on information that had been passed down through centuries. Some of the information went back as far as Greek philosopher Aristotle (384–322 B.C.). One popular belief was that everything in the world was made up of four elements—air, water, fire, and earth—in different proportions. Some scientists thought that the elements could be changed or "transmuted" into one another. Others believed that everything but air came from water.

Scientists were also beginning to learn about compounds, substances made up of two or more elements. They knew that elements like copper and gold combined in specific proportions, but they did not understand why or how. In those days, a scientific event that could not be explained was dismissed as "magic" or "superstition."

Lavoisier was not like the other scientists. He could not dismiss what he could not explain. He believed science should be based upon proven facts, because facts did not deceive. He wrote: "I had . . . become familiar with the rigor with which mathematicians reason in their treatises. They never prove a proposition unless the preceding step has been made clear. Everything is tied together, everything is connected."[3]

Years later, Lavoisier wrote about his early study of chemistry. He said that he had "spent four years studying a science . . . founded on only a few facts, that this science was composed of absolutely incoherent ideas and unproven suppositions . . . and that it was untouched by the logic of science. I realized I would have to begin the study of chemistry all over again."[4]

In 1764, Lavoisier received his license to practice law and was admitted to the *Parlement de Paris*. The same year, the French Academy of Sciences sponsored a contest to see who had the best idea to improve city street lighting. The French Academy was the main scientific agency of France. It had been established in 1666, under the direction of the king. One of its purposes was to study scientific issues that affected the country's well-being. Members shared their research results at French Academy meetings.

Lavoisier entered the contest. As part of his study, he covered the walls of his room with dark cloth. For six weeks he lived in darkness as he tested different streetlamps. In the end he gave the French Academy a seventy-page report. One of his recommendations was that olive oil and oil pressed from other seeds could be used to light the streetlamps. Lavoisier shared the prize with three other winners. On August 9, 1766, the king awarded him a gold medal, which was presented to him by the president of the French Academy.

Lavoisier wanted to become a member of the French Academy of Sciences. He saw membership as "an honorable profession and, in a way, a public function."[5] Most scientists had to wait many years before they could become members of the French Academy of Sciences, as only a certain number were allowed membership at any one time. An opening became available only when an existing member died, and each scientist who applied had to be approved by the king.

The academy did not admit Lavoisier after he won the street-lighting contest. Not one to be easily discouraged, he continued working in his laboratory. Some of his early experiments involved the mineral gypsum, which is used to make plaster. Lavoisier analyzed gypsum and presented his results at a meeting of the French Academy. Finally, they were convinced. In 1768, when he was twenty-five years old, Lavoisier was admitted into the French Academy of Sciences.

Antoine Lavoisier with E. I. du Pont

One of Antoine Lavoisier's students, Éleuthère Irénée du Pont, left France and came to America, where his last name became a household word.

Born in Paris in 1771, E. I. du Pont was the youngest son of Pierre-Samuel du Pont de Nemours, a government official. Du Pont was interested in gunpowder from an early age. When he was fourteen years old, he wrote a paper on gunpowder. Later his father helped him get a job with the Gunpowder and Saltpeter Administration. There he worked and studied gunpowder manufacture with Lavoisier.

After the French Revolution, du Pont and his older brother Victor emigrated to the United States with their father. Du Pont found American gunpowder to be of poor quality. Using the modern procedures he had learned from Lavoisier, du Pont opened a gunpowder manufacturing plant near Wilmington, Delaware. He named his plant Lavoisier Mills after his mentor and teacher. Later its name was changed to E. I. Du Pont de Nemours and Company.

Du Pont's gunpowder supplied the United States during the Mexican War, the British during the Crimean War, and the Northern states during the Civil War. Eventually the company branched out into the manufacture of blasting powder (dynamite), used to open iron and coal mines.

E.I. du Pont was a charitable man who gave much money to the poor and blind. He was also in favor of free public education. He died in Philadelphia in 1834.

Du Pont de Nemours and Company rose to become one of the largest chemical companies in the world. Today, Du Pont employs over 55,000 people worldwide. It is a major U.S. manufacturer of many items used in the home and workplace. Some of the products Du Pont produces include Teflon resin coatings, Lycra spandex fibers, and Stainmaster stain-resistant carpets.

Joseph Black was a Scottish chemist who identified the chemical properties of carbon dioxide (CO_2) in 1754.

3

Oxygen,
Not Phlogiston

In 1767, Guettard once again asked Lavoisier to go with him on a scientific trip. The two scientists traveled by horseback through the Vosges Mountains, near the Swiss border. They studied soils and classified rock fragments. They also examined drinking water and mineral water. Lavoisier was convinced that the content of mineral water reflected the soil from which it came. This was the beginning of Lavoisier's interest in water. Later in his career, he would study it in great detail.

By this time, Lavoisier had chosen science over law as his life's work. When he was twenty-five years old, he inherited money from his mother's and grandmother's estates. In March 1768, he invested his inheritance in a private company called the General Farm, also known as the Tax Farm. The company worked with France's controller-general of finance to collect taxes for the king on salt, tobacco, alcohol, and imports. Without having to worry about earning money, Lavoisier was able to devote himself to science.

Lavoisier became a regional inspector for the Tobacco Commission. His supervisor, Jacques Paulze, was an honest man who expected the same from Lavoisier. However, not all of the Farmers General, as they were called, were as honest as Paulze and Lavoisier.

Although it provided a good income, tax collection was not a very popular line of work. The common people resented the Farmers General. While the collectors were not members of the aristocracy, they were educated and prosperous men. Their elegant homes and lifestyles reminded the lower class that all was not equal in eighteenth-century French society.

Paulze was a widower with a fourteen-year-old daughter named Marie-Anne Pierrette. She was petite and lovely, with a mane of brown hair and intense blue eyes. She had gone to a convent school. Like Lavoisier, she was curious about the world around her. She also had musical talent, and played both the harp and the harpsichord. Lavoisier found Marie easy to talk to, and a friendship developed between them. He told her of his scientific studies and of his travels as a Farmer General.

Other men were interested in Marie, and one in particular, the Comte d'Amerval, wanted to marry her. He was fifty years old and had no money. Marie did not want to marry him. She called him a "fool, an unfeeling rustic and an ogre."[1]

Paulze's supervisor at the Tobacco Commission was Abbé Terray, the controller-general of finance. Terray was also Paulze's uncle by marriage, and a friend of d'Amerval's. Terray thought Paulze should force Marie to marry d'Amerval. He threatened to fire Paulze from the Tobacco Commission if she did not. Despite Terray's threats, Paulze refused to push Marie into marriage. He wrote to Terray: "I can see, sir, no advantages in this marriage. The count is fifty years old, my daughter, fourteen. He is penniless and . . . his character is scarcely suited to that of a young convent-bred girl. Furthermore, my daughter has a decided aversion to him and I will not force her to marry him!"[2]

Paulze knew he had put off Terray and d'Amerval for just a short while. The only way to permanently ruin their plans was to find another man for Marie to marry. Paulze thought Lavoisier would make a good husband for Marie, and Lavoisier agreed. Marie was pleased with her father's choice of husband. She and Lavoisier were both intelligent, shared the same interests, and enjoyed spending time together. They were married on December 16, 1771, and moved into a home in Paris bought for them by Lavoisier's father.

From the very beginning of their marriage, Madame Lavoisier supported her husband's interest in science. To be of help to him, she studied chemistry and worked as his research assistant. Sitting to the side of the lab, she would record the results shouted out to her. She taught herself English and translated the experiments of other scientists for Lavoisier. She also learned Latin so as to be able to read very old scientific reports written in this language. She served as her husband's secretary, helping him answer letters from scientists all over the world.

Lavoisier was successful as a Farmer General. His high income allowed Madame Lavoisier to make their home comfortable and fashionable. Their furnishings were the most modern in style and color. Many scientists, politicians, and other important people visited the Lavoisiers. Madame Lavoisier was a gracious hostess who made her visitors feel welcome. French scientist Antoine-François de Fourcroy (1755–1809) wrote: "I shall never in my life forget the privileged hours which I spent [at the Lavoisiers'] where it was so pleasant for me to attend."[3] American scientist and statesman Benjamin Franklin (1706–1790), living in Paris as the American ambassador to France, often visited the Lavoisiers.

Madame Lavoisier took art lessons from painter Jacques-Louis David (1748–1825). Soon she was illustrating Lavoisier's laboratory reports and books. She painstakingly created thirteen plates that were included in Lavoisier's book *Elementary Treatise of Chemistry*. She also painted as a hobby. She especially liked depicting Franklin. Thanking her for one of the paintings, Franklin wrote to Madame Lavoisier: "It is allowed by those who have seen it to have great merit as a picture in every respect; but what particularly endears it to me, is the hand that drew it."[4]

Antoine-François de Fourcroy was one of the four "French Chemists" who worked with Lavoisier revising chemical nomenclature. After the French Revolution, he became an advocate for higher education.

As an inspector for the Tax Farm, Lavoisier traveled the Marne, Champagne, and Ardennes regions of France. As he conducted tax business, he also studied the minerals of the places he visited. From his observations, Lavoisier drew sixteen maps; these were included in a mineralogy atlas that was published in 1770.

Lavoisier divided his time among the Tax Farm, his own personal scientific research, and the research he conducted for the French Academy of Sciences. One of the youngest scientists at the French Academy, he was eager to investigate all subjects. His first assignment was to investigate ways of providing Paris with fresh drinking water. When the members of the academy disagreed over the best way to analyze the water, Lavoisier designed an experiment to study the nature of water itself.

At the time, scientists believed that earth and water were interchangeable. Lavoisier wanted to test this theory. Using a special piece of laboratory glass-ware called a pelican, he added a measured amount of clean rainwater, sealed it, and boiled it for 101 days. When the boiling was complete, there were white flakes in the water. He weighed the flakes as he had been taught by his early teacher, La Caille. He found that the flakes came from the container, not from the water itself. Water could not be changed into earth, Lavoisier told the French Academy.

Either alone or with other scientists, Lavoisier wrote and presented over 200 scientific reports for the French Academy. He studied the soap-making and coal-mining industries, and recommended how they could be made more productive and profitable. He investigated prisons and hospitals and suggested better ways to care for prisoners and patients. He often used his own money to finance his studies. Most of his suggestions were ignored by the French government.

One of Lavoisier's personal scientific interests had to do with air and the part it played in burning, or combustion. At the time he was studying air, other scientists knew it was involved in combustion, but they were not sure how. Using a large magnifying glass called a burning lens, Lavoisier heated some diamonds. He found that when they were heated in a vacuum, they remained "absolutely unchanged." When they were heated in the presence of air, they were destroyed.

Next Lavoisier burned phosphorous and sulfur. These are two nonmetals that are found throughout nature. The burning experiments showed that air was necessary for combustion. The experiments also showed that when phosphorous and sulfur were heated, they were turned into acids that were heavier than the non-heated form.

Shortly before Lavoisier began his studies of air, another French scientist, Louis-Bernard Guyton de Morveau (1737–1816), had proved that metals subjected to high heat were changed into a powdery ash. The ash, called calx, weighed more than the original metal. The process of producing calx is called calcination. Lavoisier knew that calcination could also be reversed. When the calx was heated with charcoal, it was brought back to the metal. (This process is called reducing.) When a calx was reduced, bubbles appeared. Only a gas can produce bubbles. Lavoisier described the bubbles coming from the calx as "a sudden discharge of the air that was somehow dissolved in them."[5] He believed that air entered the calx as it was being formed, causing an increase in weight. When the calx was reduced, the air was released in bubbles.

Lavoisier further studied the process of calcining. He reduced lead oxide with charcoal. Using a specially designed apparatus, he collected a large amount of air given off during the reduction. Each time he repeated the experiment, the calx weighed more than the original lead oxide.

While Lavoisier was conducting these experiments on lead oxide, much of the scientific community believed that fire contained an invisible substance called phlogiston. Phlogiston had been proposed in 1703 by German scientist George Ernst Stahl (1660–1734). Stahl theorized that every combustible substance contained phlogiston, and that phlogiston was released when the substance was burned. Phlogiston was believed to be the chemical ingredient of fire that was released in the flame.

The results of Lavoisier's lead oxide experiments did not agree with the phlogiston theory. If an element lost phlogiston when calx was formed, the calx should weigh less than the original substance, not more. Lavoisier's samples, however, weighed more after burning. Phlogiston supporters claimed that the phlogiston left the metal and entered the calx, causing the calx to weigh more. Lavoisier had a different explanation. He suggested that the extra weight in the calx came from air, which in some way combined with the calx. When the calx was reduced, the air was released as bubbles.

Lavoisier developed his experiments one step further. He calcined tin in sealed vessels called retorts. When calcination was complete and the retort was opened, Lavoisier heard the sound of air rushing into the vessel. This could only mean that a vacuum had formed in the retort; the original air in the retort had been used up in the calcination. Lavoisier measured the air that rushed into the retort. He observed that the increase in the tin's weight was equal to the weight of air that entered the vessel after it had been opened. This proved to Lavoisier that it was air, not phlogiston, that combined with the calx to give it its extra weight.

Lavoisier realized that his theory, if accepted, would have a huge impact on science. To insure that he was given proper credit for his work, on November 1, 1772, Lavoisier recorded his experiments, placed the record in a sealed envelope, and gave it to the secretary of the French Academy. "Since this discovery seemed to me to be one of the most interesting that had been made since Stahl's, I felt that I ought to ensure that it remained my property," Lavoisier wrote.[6] With these words, modern chemistry was born. On February 20, 1773, he wrote in his laboratory notebook that his experiments "seemed to me destined to bring about a revolution in physics and chemistry."[7] Lavoisier included these experiments in his book, *Physical and Chemical Essay*, which was published in 1774. It was a chemistry book unlike any published before, and Lavoisier's name became well-known in the field of chemistry.

Lavoisier's combustion experiments opened up a new world of scientific study, but he knew there was still much to be done. "An immense series of experiments remains to be made," he wrote in his laboratory notebook.[8]

Once he had proven that air was involved in calcination, Lavoisier wanted to find out what air was made of. Scientists knew that atmospheric air (also called common air) was some kind of gas, but they did not know whether it was one gas or a mixture of several gases. Lavoisier was particularly interested in learning the nature of the gas that combined with calx.

Other scientists were also studying what was loosely referred to as "airs." In 1754, Scottish chemist Joseph Black (1728–1799) saw gas released when he placed chalk in acid. Black named the gas "fixed air," because he thought it was "fixed" or in some way attached to the chalk. Further experiments had proven that fixed air was different from atmospheric air. It did not make a candle burn. Animals forced to breathe fixed air did not survive. Lavoisier wanted to know whether it was fixed air or atmospheric air that combined with calx to give it its additional weight.

Joseph Priestley (1733–1804), a British scientist and minister, was also studying "airs." He had found that when a calx of mercury was reduced, a gas purer than atmospheric air was produced. "What surprised me more than I can well express was, that a candle burnt in this air with a remarkably vigorous [strong] flame," Priestley observed.[9] Priestly could not identify the gas, so he called it dephlogisticated air—he assumed that the candle's flame burned brighter because it absorbed phlogiston. When Priestley himself breathed this dephlogisticated air, his "breast felt peculiarly light and easy for some time afterwards."[10]

In October 1774, Priestley visited Lavoisier and described his mercury calx experiments to him. Shortly thereafter, Lavoisier repeated Priestley's experiments. When he reduced the calx with charcoal, "fixed air" was produced. When he reduced the calx with heat alone, however, he found he had produced Priestley's dephlogisticated air. Lavoisier renamed dephlogisticated air, calling it "eminently respirable" (meaning "extremely easy to breathe") air. He described it as being "pure air, more breathable, if it can be said, than atmospheric air and more likely to sustain flames and the combustion of bodies."[11]

Charcoal had not been used in the reduction that produced the respirable gas. Lavoisier concluded that the gas came from the calx itself. Additional experiments proved it was respirable air that combined with metals during calcination. Lavoisier believed that respirable air was part of atmospheric air, and that it was also responsible for combustion. He also discovered that calcining caused another type of air to be formed. This air could not be breathed or combusted. Lavoisier called this "azote," which comes from the Greek word meaning "no life."

More research on air followed. Lavoisier showed that respirable air makes up about 20 percent of atmospheric gas. He proved that Black's "fixed air" was really a compound of carbon and respirable air. He showed that respirable air and azote mixed in the proper proportions produce atmospheric air. Fixed air is known today as carbon dioxide; it is the gas that we exhale when we breathe. Azote would eventually be renamed nitrogen.

Lavoisier discovered that respirable air was used up whenever carbon, phosphorous, or sulfur was burned. When the products of these combustions were dissolved in water, they were found to be acidic. Lavoisier thought that respirable air was found in all acids, a theory that was later proven incorrect.

In late 1774, Lavoisier announced his findings. "I believe I am in a position to confirm that air, however pure one can suppose it to be . . . far from being a simple . . . element, as has been commonly thought, must on the contrary be placed at least in the mixed class, and perhaps even in the compound one."[12] He gave no credit to Priestley in his study.

Lavoisier's announcement that he had discovered respirable air angered Priestly. Priestly accused Lavoisier of stealing his idea. "After I left Paris, I procured the [mercury calx]. . . . [I] had spoken of the experiments that I had made, and that I had intended to make with it, he [Lavoisier] began his experiments upon the same substance, and presently found what I have called dephlogisticated air," Priestley accused.[13]

English scientist Joseph Priestly studied oxygen with an apparatus such as this. He accused Lavoisier of plagiarizing his experimental results. Although Priestly was among the first to discover oxygen, it was Lavoisier who realized its importance.

Lavoisier argued Priestley's claims and insisted he had begun his research in April 1774. He later admitted that he did not start the combustion tests on mercury until November 1774.

Scientists now believe that neither Lavoisier nor Priestly discovered the new gas. In 1772, Swedish scientist Carl Wilhelm Scheele (1742–1786) discovered what he called "fire air." It was later shown to be the same as Priestley's dephlogisticated air and Lavoisier's respirable air. However, because Scheele did not publish his experiments until after Priestly and Lavoisier made their claims, he is often overlooked as the discoverer.

Regardless of who gets credit for finding the new gas, Lavoisier was the first to identify it, demonstrate its quantity in atmospheric air, and show its importance. He was also the first to give it a name. Believing (incorrectly) that all acids were compounds of respirable air, in 1779, Lavoisier renamed the gas *principe oxygine*, which means "acid former." We know it today as oxygen.

Carl Wilheim Scheele discovered oxygen two years prior to Priestly and Lavoisier, but failed to publish his discovery. Here one of his scientific illustrations details an experiment with oxygen.

Benjamin Franklin

Antoine Lavoisier and Benjamin Franklin shared much in common. They were both scientists who also served as statesmen. Both were patriotic men who loved their countries. Both strove to improve the lives of their fellow countrymen.

Franklin was almost seventy years old when he was sent to France by the Second Continental Congress. His mission was to obtain aid for the American colonies, which were at war with the British. Franklin asked France for soldiers, money, and gunpowder.

The two scientists met in 1776. Franklin was a frequent guest at Lavoisier's home. He often accompanied Lavoisier to meetings of the French Academy of Sciences. Sometimes he assisted academy members with experiments. As a result of his work with electricity, Franklin was made an honorary member of the academy.

Franklin was popular in France. His role in the formation of the new American government was well known. There was a picture of him in almost every Parisian home. While in Paris, Franklin was active in society. He took part in all aspects of French culture, including learning the language and attending theatrical performances. He also kept up with his personal interests of science and printing.

Franklin possessed a cheerful personality that made him easy to like, and he was a good negotiator. France and Great Britain had been enemies for a long time. The French government was happy to help the American colonies in their struggle for independence from Great Britain. There is no question that without the money, soldiers, supplies, and gunpowder that France gave the colonies, the United States would have never won the Revolutionary War. "One can truly say that North America owes its independence to French gunpowder," Lavoisier wrote in 1789.[14]

Franklin served as the U.S. ambassador to France for seven and one half years. In 1784, he was replaced by Thomas Jefferson. The people of France never forgot Benjamin Franklin. When he died in 1790, France, now governed by the National Assembly, declared three days of public mourning.

In 1766, Henry Cavendish discovered "inflammable air," which he believed was pure phlogiston. Lavoisier used Cavendish's studies to disprove the phlogiston theory.

4

A Scientific Revolution

Controversy over who discovered oxygen was not the only argument Lavoisier was involved in during the late 1770s and early 1780s. His combustion theory itself was met with lively debate everywhere, including within the French Academy. The scientists usually sat politely as fellow members read scientific papers. When Lavoisier presented his *Reflections of Phlogiston* in 1783, they protested loudly. Calling phlogiston "an imaginary entity," Lavoisier read: "[C]hemists have made phlogiston a vague principle which is not strictly defined and which consequently fits all the explanations required of it; sometimes the principle has weight, sometimes it has not; sometimes it is free fire, sometimes it is fire combined with earth; sometimes it passes through the pores of vessels, sometimes these are impenetrable to it; . . . [it] changes its form at every instant."[1]

One objection to Lavoisier's theory was that it could not explain the gas that Henry Cavendish (1731–1810) had discovered in England in 1766. Cavendish called his gas "inflammable air" because it was easy to burn. (Inflammable air was later renamed hydrogen.) Cavendish believed inflammable air was pure phlogiston. When it was burned in a vessel, tiny drops of a clear liquid were produced. Cavendish called the liquid "dew," and later showed it was water.

Lavoisier believed water was not an element, but a compound that formed when oxygen and hydrogen combined. In 1783, he repeated Cavendish's experiments. Lavoisier was able to separate the two gases when he heated iron with water. The hydrogen was released and the oxygen combined with the iron calx. These experiments were additional proof that phlogiston did not exist. A little at a time, scientists began to agree with Lavoisier's combustion theory.

In his next set of experiments, Lavoisier studied heat and respiration. He had long believed that combustion and respiration were similar processes. They both used up oxygen and gave off carbon dioxide. Now he wanted to see if both processes generated the same amount of heat. A colleague, Pierre-Simon de Laplace (1749–1827), helped Lavoisier with the respiration experiments.

Pierre-Simon de Laplace designed the calorimeter that Lavoisier used in his respiration experiments.

Laplace had designed a piece of laboratory equipment called a calorimeter, which detects heat from various sources, including the body of an animal. An animal's body produces enough heat to melt ice. The calorimeter detects heat by measuring the amount of water formed when the ice melts. Using guinea pigs, Lavoisier and Laplace measured how much oxygen the animals breathed in and how much carbon dioxide they breathed out. They then measured how much water the animal's body heat produced from a known weight of ice. Next they determined how much charcoal was needed to melt the same amount of ice and produce the same amount of carbon dioxide on combustion. These experiments showed that Lavoisier was correct: respiration and combustion were similar processes. Later, Lavoisier learned that two separate reactions occurred during respiration. One produced carbon dioxide, and one produced hydrogen.

Many years later, Lavoisier repeated his respiration experiments on humans, using a young scientist named Armand Seguin (1767–1835). While Seguin breathed in pure oxygen, Lavoisier measured his uptake of the gas, as well as the man's heartbeat and rate of breathing. He measured these things again while Seguin performed a variety of activities. He found that Seguin used more oxygen when he was working than he did when resting. Lavoisier reported his findings to the French Academy in 1790. He told the academy that the fuel needed for the combustion of respiration comes from the food the animal (or human) eats. When the fuel is used up, the animal will die, Lavoisier explained.

While Lavoisier was working on his chemistry experiments, he was also working as a tax collector. He wrote reports for the Tax Farm and managed expenses. He also managed Tax Farm employees. He traveled widely. He was always observing the lower classes and looking for ways to improve their lives.

In 1775 Lavoisier and four other men were appointed to France's Gunpowder and Saltpeter Administration. Lavoisier was selected because he was a well-known chemist who had shown good judgment while working for the Tax Farm. Gunpowder was sorely needed by France to protect itself and its colonies. The Seven Years' War (1756–1763) between England and France, of which the French and Indian War in the American colonies was a part, had depleted France's supply. The commissioners were put in charge of making more and better gunpowder.

As a commissioner, Lavoisier worked to improve the gunpowder manu-facturing process. He also found better ways to make saltpeter (also known as potassium nitrate), one of gunpowder's components. He taught chemistry and mathematics to those who manufactured the gunpowder. The workers were not always happy about the changes Lavoisier wanted to make. In the end, however, because of Lavoisier's methods, many new gunpowder and saltpeter factories were built. Soon France had plenty of good-quality gunpowder. There was even enough to sell to other countries, including the American colonies, which were fighting for their freedom from England.

The Lavoisiers moved into an apartment in the Gunpowder Arsenal Complex, where the gunpowder was stored. The arsenal was near the Bastille, overlook-ing the Seine River. For the next seventeen years, the Lavoisiers lived at the arsenal. Madame Lavoisier turned the dreary apartment into an elegant home. Once again the Lavoisiers entertained the noted and powerful. Madame Lavoisier gave a dinner party each Monday evening. The couple was active socially and attended the opera and art exhibits.

Although he was a gunpowder commissioner, Lavoisier continued working with the Tax Farm and conducting his scientific experiments. He designed and built a new chemistry lab at the arsenal. With its modern gasometers, barom-eters, balances, and hydrometers, it soon became one of the best equipped laboratories in Europe. Many scientists, young and old, came to observe Lavoisier and work with him in the lab. Lavoisier kept a rigid work schedule. He and Madame Lavoisier rose at five in the morning and worked together in the lab from six to nine. Lavoisier then attended meetings at the Tax Farm. His afternoons were divided between the Gunpowder Administration and the French Academy of Sciences. After a quick supper, he and Madame Lavoisier returned to the lab and worked from seven to ten in the evening.

Lavoisier spent Saturdays with his students. "For him," Madame Lavoisier later wrote, "it was a blissful day. A few enlightened friends, a few young people, considering it an honor to be able to participate in his experiments, gathered in the laboratory in the morning. It was there that they ate lunch, discussed, and created the theory that immortalized its author. It was there that one had to see and hear that man whose mind was so sound, talent so pure and genius so lofty. It was from his conversation there that the nobility of his moral principles could be judged."[2]

In 1778, the Lavoisiers bought Frechines, a farm and country home near Blois, outside of Paris. Lavoisier had always been interested in agriculture. A farm of his own gave him a chance to try out some of his ideas on farming.

Lavoisier's farming techniques merged chemistry and agriculture. He taught the peasants living on his farm how to rotate their crops. He introduced them to new crops, such as the potato. He showed them the value of manure, and of feeding farm animals hay to cut down on food costs. Word of Lavoisier's farming success spread to the newly formed United States of America. George Washington sought Lavoisier's advice for Mount Vernon, his farm in Virginia. Lavoisier's agricultural experiments were so successful that King Louis XVI ordered a committee of agriculture be formed, and he named Lavoisier as chairman. "Agriculture is the most important of all factories. . . . [I]t is consequently, the almost unique source of all the national wealth," Lavoisier wrote.[3]

French society placed Lavoisier above the lower classes, but Lavoisier cared a great deal about the common people. He had been studying the peasants and farmers of France since his first trip through the Vosges Mountains with Guettard in 1767. He saw that their lives were a daily struggle, and he helped when he could. He loaned farmers money when they did not have a good growing season. When crops failed in 1788 and the farmers were starving, Lavoisier gave them money to purchase wheat. He also wanted to see the lower classes provided for in their old age. He convinced the French government to set up an insurance fund that would allow farmers to invest a small part of their earnings each year. Then, when they were too old to work, the farmers could use their savings for living expenses.

Although he worked for the government as a tax collector, Lavoisier did not feel the tax laws were fair. He thought the poor people paid too much in taxes, and the rich not enough. He objected to the way tax collectors sometimes invaded a family's privacy when they were collecting taxes. As with his ideas to improve prisons and hospitals, the government ignored Lavoisier's suggestions.

One of the responsibilities of the Tax Farm was to collect taxes on goods brought into Paris from outside the city. About 20 percent of these imports were slipped in without being taxed. This was not good for the government because it lost out on the tax. It was also unfair to those Parisian shopkeepers who paid the tax. Lavoisier had an idea of how to stop this unfairness. He proposed building a wall around Paris. The wall would have gates that would be guarded so that no one could bring goods into the city without paying the tax.

In 1783, the wall was begun. It was six feet high and had sixty-six gates. The wall was very unpopular with the citizens of Paris. They said it made them feel like they were in prison. They also claimed it made them sick because it prevented them from getting fresh air. The Paris wall made many enemies for Lavoisier. One newspaper editorial called him the "vile inventor of a tyrannical project."[4]

Lavoisier made enemies in other ways also. In 1784, a group of French doctors asked the French Academy of Sciences to look into a claim by an Austrian doctor named Anton Mesmer (1734–1815). Mesmer said he could cure people of disease with a technique he developed called magnetic therapy. Mesmer believed that people had a magnetism that could be spread from one person to another.

Mesmerism was gaining popularity with the people of Paris. Doctors, however, were worried that mesmerism was hurting people instead of healing them. The French Academy formed a committee to investigate Mesmer's claim of healing. Lavoisier and Benjamin Franklin, who was living in Paris at the time, were members of the committee.

The committee saw that magnetic therapeutics often included a group of people sitting together in tubs of water poured from bottles. Mesmer claimed that the water was magnetized. The committee observed Mesmer's assistant waving a wand over the patients, which Mesmer also claimed was magnetized and helped with healing. The committee observed people when they thought they were being magnetized and when they thought they weren't.

In 1784, the committee reported to the French Academy of Sciences that magnetic therapy did not heal people or make them well. Those who believed they were being healed were so because they believed they would be. It was mind over matter. The report made those who believed in Mesmer and his techniques angry.

Louis-Bernard Guyton de Morveau was a lawyer-turned-chemist who helped Lavoisier with his early calcination experiments. He later helped with the nomenclature project.

Meanwhile, Lavoisier continued to work on his revolution in chemistry. With the French chemist Louis-Bernard Guyton de Morveau, who had done early calcination experiments, and two other chemists, Lavoisier designed a naming system for chemicals. Lavoisier wanted to standardize the names of chemical substances and place them in categories so that they would be easily recognized and remembered. Before he and his fellow scientists began this work, there was no reasoning behind the naming of chemicals. Lavoisier and his colleagues developed a chemical language that all chemists would know and understand. The new naming system told what a compound was made of, which gave scientists an idea of how it would react with other chemicals. In 1787, Lavoisier published his ideas of chemical naming in *Methods of Chemical Nomenclature.*

A few years later, in 1789, Lavoisier published *Elementary Treatise of Chemistry,* his best-known book. It became the classic chemistry textbook of the eighteenth and nineteenth centuries, and chemists throughout the world came to rely on the ideas contained in it. In *Elementary Treatise of Chemistry,* Lavoisier explains his ideas of modern chemistry. One of these ideas has to do with chemical reactions. Lavoisier stated that chemical reactions neither create nor destroy matter. He proved this by showing that the weight of the substances used to begin a reaction equaled that of the products at the end of a reaction. He wrote, "We may lay it down as an incontestable axiom, that . . . nothing is created; an equal quantity of matter exists both before and after the experiment; the quality and the quantity of the elements remain precisely the same . . . upon this principal the whole art of performing chemical experiments depends."[5] This important theory is known today as the law of the conservation of mass.

Antoine Lavoisier wanted all chemists to benefit from one another's work. For this to happen, they had to speak the same language. Before Lavoisier developed his system of chemical nomenclature [terminology], chemists from different countries used different names for the same substance. Sometimes a name had very little to do with the substance. For example, hydrochloric acid was called "spirit of salt," and sulfuric acid "spirit of vitriol."

Lavoisier believed that all things were made of either one element or many elements combined in a particular way. He wanted to develop a system in which every substance was named for what it contained.

Lavoisier's colleagues—Louis-Bernard Guyton de Morveau, Count Claude-Louis Berthollet, and Antoine de Fourcroy—helped Lavoisier develop his system. These four men became known as the French Chemists. They first tested substances to learn what was in them. Then they gave each chemical a suffix, or ending to its name. Chemicals made of two substances received an ending of -ide. For example, sodium chloride (common table salt) is made of sodium and chlorine. Compounds containing oxygen received an ending of -ate or -ite, depending upon the amount of oxygen it contained. Many other suffixes were also used.

Lavoisier published Methods of Chemical Nomenclature in 1787. It was met with much resistance. The chemical nomenclature used today was developed by the International Union of Pure and Applied Chemistry in 1921. Many of Lavoisier's ideas were incorporated into this system.

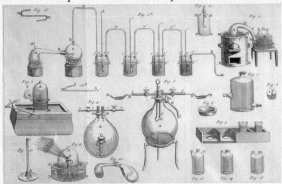

Madame Lavoisier illustrated her husband's scientific notebooks and text books with drawings similar to these.

Marie-Antoinette Lavoisier was a woman of many talents who possessed the same curious nature as her husband. She spent many hours in the lab at Lavoisier's side, recording the experimental results shouted out to her by him or one of his assistants.

Scientific Advancements of the 19th Century

5

The father of
Modern Chemistry

By the late 1780s, life was good for Antoine and Marie Lavoisier. Scientists from all over the world were beginning to realize that he was correct about phlogiston: It didn't exist. One chemist wrote: "At last I am laying down my arms and abandoning phlogiston. . . . I myself will give a refutation of my own essay on phlogiston."[1] Lavoisier's many experiments were providing the clues and answers to questions that had puzzled chemists and biologists alike. His books were furthering the "revolution in chemistry" that he had wanted to bring about. And in 1785, Lavoisier became director of the French Academy of Sciences.

The country of France, however, was in turmoil. There was no money in the treasury. In desperation, on May 5, 1979, Louis XVI called a meeting of the Estates-General, a national congress that had not met in almost 200 years. The Estates-General represented the three segments, called Estates, of French society. The clergy and members of the church were represented by the First Estate. The nobility and aristocracy were represented by the Second Estate. The Third Estate represented the middle class. The lowest class had no representation.

At the meeting, the king announced that the representatives of the Third Estate, which was the largest, would not have as much voting power as the First and Second Estates. On June 17, the angry representatives of the Third Estate rebelled against the king and changed their name to the National Assembly. Meeting on a nearby tennis court, the National Assembly vowed to write a

French constitution similar to the American Bill of Rights. A month later, the common people in Paris showed their own displeasure with the king by storming the Bastille, killing French guards and releasing prisoners.

Lavoisier knew changes had to be made in France. He wanted to see more power given to the people, but he still wanted the king to head the country. It was a system that worked in Great Britain. Lavoisier believed it could work in France also.

A few months after the Bastille was stormed, the National Assembly, which had changed its name to the National Convention, asked Lavoisier and some other scientists for help. The new government wanted to set up a standardized system of weights and measures for France. The scientists developed the metric system. This means of scientific measurement is used today by scientists throughout the world.

The National Convention gave Lavoisier other work to do. In 1791, he wrote a report on the French economy. Soon after, the National Convention closed down the Tax Farm. Even though Lavoisier had been a tax collector, the new French government asked him for help. He and five other men were put in charge of France's treasury. Lavoisier was also asked to assist the Advisory Council of Arts and Crafts. This agency helped citizens by educating them and teaching them useful trades.

Disorder and violence continued in Paris through the summer of 1791. On one August day alone, 1,400 people were killed. Lavoisier gave up all his government positions, then left his home and laboratory in the arsenal. For a while he and Madame Lavoisier stayed at their country home in Frechines, but eventually they returned to Paris.

By then Robespierre and the National Convention were ruling France and slowly doing away with everything associated with the monarchy. The new government wanted to close the French Academy of Sciences. For almost two years, Lavoisier fought to save the academy. He had been a member for twenty-four years, and had served as both its director and treasurer. "Does [the National Convention] wish to suspend investigations that it has itself initiated?" Lavoisier asked.[2] Lavoisier's arguments were useless, and in August 1793, the National Convention closed down the Academy.

A politician named Jean-Paul Marat (1743–1793) was happy to see Lavoisier defeated and the French Academy closed. In 1780 Marat had applied to become a member of the academy by submitting his own ideas on combustion. Lavoisier saw no value in his research and voted against admitting him. Marat never forgave Lavoisier. In 1791, Marat attacked the scientist in his newspaper, *The Friend of the People*, writing: "Lavoisier has no ideas of his own, so he appropriates the ideas of others. . . . I have seen him first infatuated with pure phlogiston, then ruthlessly denouncing it. . . . [He] has changed the term acid into oxygen, phlogiston into azote, . . . nitrous into nitrite and nitrate. These are his claims to immortality. Proud of his great achievements, he rests on his laurels while his parasitic followers praise him to the skies."[3]

Shortly after the French Academy of Sciences was closed, the National Convention began investigating the owners of the Tax Farm. The government accused the tax collectors of not turning in all the money they had collected. Lavoisier had been an honest tax collector; however, all the Farmers General came under suspicion. Lavoisier and his father-in-law, Jacques Paulze, were arrested and their property seized.

The days in prison were long and dreary. To make the most of his time, Lavoisier wrote two volumes of an eight-volume book on his life and his chemistry. On December 19, 1793, he wrote to Madame Lavoisier: "My career has gone well . . . I have enjoyed a happy existence . . . you have contributed to it every day by the marks of endearment which you have given me. My work is done, but you have a right to hope for a long life. I am resigned to my fate and consider that I can lose nothing that I have already gained. . . . [I]t is not utterly hopeless that we will be reunited again."[4]

Madame Lavoisier begged important people, including other scientists, for help in getting her husband and father freed. She would not, however, accept freedom for Lavoisier and not her father. "Lavoisier would be dishonored were he to allow his case to be separated from that of his companions. . . . If they die, they die innocent," she told Antoine Dupin, the investigator in charge.[5]

There were no pardons for any of the Farmers General. Eventually they were all transferred to the Conciergerie. The night before the trial, Lavoisier wrote to his cousin, "I have had a fairly long career, and above all, a happy one . . . this affair will probably save me the inconvenience of old age. I shall die in good health. . . . My chief regret is that I am unable to do more for my family. . . . Social virtues, important services to country, a useful life employed in the interest of the arts and human knowledge cannot preserve me from this dismal end; I must perish as a guilty person."[6]

39

Lavoisier and the other Farmers General were charged with stealing money from the people of France, and on May 8, 1794, they were sentenced to die. Within hours of their sentence, they were taken in special carts called tumbrels to the open square where, one by one, their heads were severed from their bodies by the guillotine. Their corpses were buried in a mass grave.

Upon hearing of Lavoisier's execution, mathematician Joseph Lagrange (1736–1813) said: "It required only a moment to sever his head . . . probably one hundred years will not suffice to produce another like it."[7]

The mathematician Joseph-Louis La Grange was one of Lavoisier's friends, He survived the French Revolution.

Madame Lavoisier was imprisoned briefly during the summer of 1794. That same summer the Reign of Terror came to an end and Robespierre faced the guillotine himself. A study of the accounts of the Farmers General showed that not only had they not cheated the government, France owed them money. By then, the citizens of France were beginning to realize what a loss to science, as well as to humanity, Lavoisier's death had been.

Eventually Madame Lavoisier reclaimed most of her money and Lavoisier's laboratory equipment. She finished the writings Lavoisier had started in prison and published them. Madame Lavoisier died in Paris in 1836. She kept her husband's memory alive until her dying day.

Lavoisier's critics say that he was better at understanding science than he was at research. He wasn't the first to discover oxygen, but he was the first to demonstrate its significance in breathing and burning. Cavendish produced water from hydrogen and oxygen; Lavoisier proved that water was a compound of these two substances. But whether he developed his own theories or built upon the work of others,

In Lavoisier's time, hydrogen was produced experimentally with equipment such as this.

Lavoisier's work was the single unifying factor that brought the science of chemistry into its own. For this he is known as the Father of Modern Chemistry.

In 1789, Lavoisier wrote, "The man of science in the silence of his laboratory . . . can . . . serve his country: by his work he . . . can diminish the sum of the evils that afflict the human race, and increase enjoyment and happiness . . . he could aspire also to that glorious title of benefactor of humanity."[8]

These words are a fitting tribute to the man who gave the world the science of chemistry.

Lavoisier conducted chemical research in his laboratory with some of these pieces of equipment.

Bastille Day

Americans celebrate their independence from England on the Fourth of July. The French people celebrate their freedom on July 14. This day is called Bastille Day. It marks the day in 1789 when an angry mob stormed the Bastille, a fortress that had been turned into a prison. The storming of the Bastille signaled the beginning of the French Revolution.

Storming of Bastille by Jean-Pierre Houel

The Bastille had been built to protect King Charles V against the Burgundians in the 1300s. Over the years it became a state prison for anyone accused of committing a crime against the monarchy. By 1789, many French citizens had been jailed on the whim of the king, Louis XVI, his wife, Marie Antoinette, or any of the other members of the aristocracy. Some prisoners spent 30 or more years in the Bastille. Many wasted away and died there.

The Bastille held only seven prisoners when it was overtaken by the mob. They were released, and the prison was demolished by the crowd over several days. Only a bronze column marks the site where the Bastille once stood. Attacking the fortress was a political statement. Like the American Declaration of Independence, it told the king that his subjects would no longer be oppressed by him or his ruling class.

The Americans' successful fight for independence gave the French the courage to fight for their own freedom. And like Americans, the French people mark Bastille Day with parades, picnics, and other celebrations.

Chronology

1743	Antoine-Laurent Lavoisier is born in Paris on August 26
1754	Enters College Mazarin
1763	First mineralogy trip with Jean-Étienne Guettard
1764	Receives license to practice law and joins *Parlement de Paris*
1766	Receives gold medal for report on street lighting; presents first gypsum studies to French Academy of Sciences
1768	Using gypsum, invents plaster of Paris; becomes a member of the French Academy of Sciences; invests in Farmers General; becomes an inspector for the Tobacco Commission
1770	Reports to French Academy of Sciences that water cannot be changed into earth; begins three-year study on process of calcination; a mineralogy atlas that includes 16 of his maps is published
1771	Marries Marie Paulze
1774	Meets Joseph Priestley; publishes first book, *Physical and Chemical Essays*; announces discovery of "respirable air"
1775	Appointed commissioner to Gunpowder and Saltpeter Administration
1778	Buys country home and begins agriculture experiments
1779	Names "respirable air" oxygen
1780	With Pierre-Simon de Laplace, proves respiration is a form of combustion
1783	Formally challenges phlogiston theory; repeats Henry Cavendish's experiments; recommends building a wall around Paris to prevent illegal imports; construction of the wall is begun
1784	Studies Mesmer's magnetic therapy and finds no merits in it
1785	Becomes director of the French Academy of Sciences
1787	Working with three other scientists, describes a new chemical language; publishes ideas of chemical language in *Method of Chemical Nomenclature*
1789	French Revolution begins with the storming of the Bastille on July 14
1789	Publishes *Elementary Treatise of Chemistry*
1790	Reports results of respiration experiments to French Academy of Sciences
1791	Prepares economic report for the National Convention; with others, is put in charge of France's new government's treasury; appointed to Advisory Council of Arts and Crafts;; project to reform weights and measures results in standardized metric system
1793	Lavoisier is imprisoned; French Academy of Sciences is closed
1794	Executed on May 8 in Paris
1836	Marie Lavoisier dies on February 10 in Paris

43

Timeline of Discovery

c. 450 b.c.	Empedocles, a Greek philosopher, proposes that all matter is a combination of only four elements—air, water, earth and fire. This theory is accepted by Aristotle.
1620	Francis Bacon develops the scientific method of reasoning.
1703	George Ernst Stahl proposes phlogiston theory.
1742	Anders Celsius names a system for temperature determination.
1754	Joseph Black describes the chemical properties of carbon dioxide.
1766	Henry Cavendish discovers hydrogen.
1770–1771	Guyton de Morveau shows that metals subjected to high heat are transformed into a powdery ash.
1772	Carl Wilheim Scheele discovers oxygen which he calls "fire air."
1774	Joseph Priestley discovers oxygen, which he calls "dephlogisticated air" and which is later found to be identical to Scheele's "fire air." Antoine Lavoisier shows the importance of oxygen in breathing and combustion.
1781	Henry Cavendish shows water to be a compound.
1783	Antoine Lavoisier disproves the existence of phlogiston.
1808	John Dalton proposes the modern model of the atom.
1861	Friedrich Kekulé defines organic chemistry as the chemistry of carbon compounds.
1866	Alfred Nobel invents dynamite.
1869	Dmitri Mendeleyev arranges the known chemical elements into the periodic table.
1897	Sir Joseph J. Thompson discovers the electron.
1898	Marie Curie and Pierre Curie discover radium and polonium; M. Curie is the first to use the term *radioactive*.
1919	Ernest Rutherford discovers the proton.
1932	James Chadwick proves the existence of the neutron.
1936	Hans Adolf Krebs discovers the Krebs cycle of respiration.
1938	Otto Hahn and Lise Meitner discover atomic fission.
1939	Linus Pauling publishes *The Nature of the Chemical Bond*.
1953	James Watson and Francis Crick demonstrate a model of DNA.
1986	John Polanyi, Dudley Herschbach, and Yuan T. Lee receive Nobel Prize for their studies of chemical-reaction dynamics.
1992	Rudolph A. Marcus develops the theory of electron transfer reactions in chemical systems.
1995	Paul Crutzen, Mario Molina, and F. Sherwood Rowland receive Nobel Prize in Chemistry for their work on the formation and decomposition of ozone.
1998	Neutrinos are found to have mass, challenging the modern idea of atomic structure that states that these subatomic particles are weightless.
2003	Roderick Mackinnon discovers the structure and mechanism of ion channels.
2004	Researchers at Hamilton College have identified several methods for determining the structures and thermodynamic values for the formation of atmospheric water clusters, which scientists speculate may accelerate global warming.

Chapter Notes

Chapter One   An Accused Criminal

1. Sydney J. French, *Torch and Crucible; the Life and Death of Antoine Lavoisier* (Princeton: Princeton University Press, 1941), p. 252.

Chapter Two   Ambitious Antoine

1. Jean-Pierre Poirier, *Lavoisier: Chemist, Biologist, Economist,* translated by Rebecca Balinski (Philadelphia: University of Pennsylvania Press, 1996), p. 7.

2. Ibid., p. 8.

3. Arthur Donovan, *Antoine Lavoisier* (Oxford, England: Blackwell Publishers, 1993), p. 47.

4. Ibid.

5. Poirier, p. 13.

Chapter Three   Oxygen, Not Phlogiston

1. Arthur Donovan, *Antoine Lavoisier* (Oxford, England: Blackwell Publishers, 1993), p. 111.

2. Sydney J. French, *Torch and Crucible; the Life and Death of Antoine Lavoisier* (Princeton: Princeton University Press, 1941), p. 55.

3. Donovan, p. 166.

4. Michael White, *Acid Tongues and Tranquil Dreamers* (New York: HarperCollins, 2001), p. 69.

5. Jean-Pierre Poirier, *Lavoisier: Chemist, Biologist, Economist,* translated by Rebecca Balinski (Philadelphia: University of Pennsylvania Press, 1996), p. 55.

6. Ibid., p. 66.

7. John Hudson, *The History of Chemistry* (New York: Chapman and Hall, 1992), p. 66.

8. Ibid.

9. Ibid, p. 56.

10. Ibid, p. 57.

11. Poirier, p. 80.

12. Ibid., p. 78.

13. Ibid., p. 80.

14. Donovan, p. 199.

Chapter Four   A Scientific Revolution

1. John Hudson, *The History of Chemistry* (New York: Chapman and Hall, 1992), p. 68.

2. Jean-Pierre Poirier, *Lavoisier: Chemist, Biologist, Economist,* translated by Rebecca Balinski (Philadelphia: University of Pennsylvania Press, 1996), p. 95.

3. Ibid., p. 202.

4. Ibid., p. 172.

5. Antoine-Laurent Lavoisier, *Elementary Treatise of Chemistry,* translated by Robert Kerr (New York: Dover Publications, Inc., 1965), p. 131.

Chapter Five   The Father of Modern Chemistry

1. Eric John Holmyard, *Makers of Chemistry* (London: Oxford University Press, 1931), p. 211.

2. Arthur Donovan, *Antoine Lavoisier* (Oxford, England: Blackwell Publishers, 1993), p. 291.

3. Sydney J. French, *Torch and Crucible; the Life and Death of Antoine Lavoisier* (Princeton: Princeton University Press, 1941), p. 206.

4. Ibid., p. 246.

5. Douglas McKie, *Antoine Lavoisier: Scientist, Economist, Social Reformer* (New York: Henry Schuman, 1952), p. 393.

6. French, p. 253.

7. McKie, p. 407.

8. Ibid, p. 352.

Glossary

acid (AS-id)—a chemical compound containing hydrogen.

aristocracy (air-ih-STOCK-rah-see)—the upper and ruling class.

azote (A-zote)—the early name for nitrogen, the part of air discovered by Lavoisier that could not be breathed or used in combustion.

bourgeoisie (burz-wah-ZEE)—the middle class.

burning lens (bur-NING lenz)—a piece of glass used to heat substances by magnifying the rays of the sun.

calcination (cal-sih-NAY-shin)—the process of allowing metals to interact with oxygen, producing a calx.

calx (*pl* calces, CAL-sees)—a powdery substance that results from calcination. Metal calces are called oxides.

combustion (cum-BUS-chin)—another name for burning.

compound (KOM-pownd)—a chemical substance made from two or more elements.

element (EL-eh-ment)—a substance that cannot be broken down further by a chemical reaction.

fixed air (FIXS-ed ayr)—early name for carbon dioxide.

geology (gee-AH-luh-jee)—the study of the earth and what it is made of.

guillotine (GEE-ah-teen)—a machine used to execute criminals; it contains a sharp blade that cuts off the head.

matter (MAT-ter)—anything that takes up space and has weight.

mineralogy (mih-nih-RAH-luh-jee)—the study of rocks and minerals.

monarchy (MAH-nar-kee)—a government run by a king or queen.

nomenclature (NO-men-CLAY-chure)—a system of naming.

oxide (OK-side)—a metal compound that has reacted with oxygen.

pelican (PEL-i-can)—a piece of laboratory glassware so called because its curved, narrow upper part resembles the neck of a pelican.

phlogiston (flow-JIS-tun)—a chemical substance believed to exist in fire. Lavoisier disproved its existence.

republic (re-PUB-lik)—a type of government in which the officials are elected.

respiration (res-peh-RAY-shun)—another word for breathing. In the process of respiration, compounds containing carbon obtained from food combine with oxygen. The result is heat, water, and carbon dioxide.

saltpeter (solt-PEE-ter)—also known as potassium nitrite; one of the components used in the manufacture of gunpowder.

vacuum (VAC-yoom)—absence of air.

46

For Further Reading

For Young Adults

Balchin, John. *100 Scientists Who Changed the World*. New York: Enchanted Lion Books, 2003.

Bragg, Melvyn. *On Giants' Shoulders*. London: Hodder and Stoughton, 1998.

Grey, Vivian. *The Chemist Who Lost His Head: The Story of Antoine Laurent Lavoisier*. New York: Coward, McCann and Geoghegan, Inc. 1982.

Kramer, Stephen P. *How to Think Like a Scientist: Answering Questions by the Scientific Method*. New York: HarperCollins Juvenile Books, 1987.

Yount, Lisa. *Antoine Lavoisier, Founder of Modern Chemistry*. Berkeley Heights, NJ: Enslow Publishers, 1997.

Works Consulted

Donovan, Arthur. *Antoine Lavoisier*. Oxford, England: Blackwell Publishers, 1993.

French, Sydney J. *Torch and Crucible; the Life and Death of Antoine Lavoisier*. Princeton: Princeton University Press, 1941.

Holmes, Frederic Lawrence. *Lavoisier and the Chemistry of Life: An Exploration of Scientific Creativity*. Madison: University of Wisconsin Press, 1985.

———. *Antoine Lavoisier: The Next Crucial Year*. Princeton: Princeton University Press, 1998.

Holmyard, Eric John. *Makers of Chemistry*. London: Oxford University Press, 1931.

Hudson, John. *The History of Chemistry*. New York: Chapman and Hall, 1992.

Lacroix, Paul. *France in the Eighteenth Century: Its Institutions, Customs, and Costumes*. New York: Frederick Ungar Publishing Co., 1963.

Lavoisier, Antoine-Laurent. *Elementary Treatise of Chemistry* (translated by Robert Kerr). New York: Dover Publications, Inc., 1965.

McKie, Douglas. *Antoine Lavoisier: Scientist, Economist, Social Reformer*. New York: Henry Schuman, 1952.

Poirier, Jean-Pierre. *Lavoisier: Chemist, Biologist, Economist* (translated by Rebecca Balinski). Philadelphia: University of Pennsylvania Press, 1996.

White, Michael. *Acid Tongues and Tranquil Dreamers*. New York: HarperCollins, 2001.

On the Internet

Biographies of Antoine Lavoisier:
http://historyofscience.free.fr/Lavoisier-Friends/a_contents_lavoisier.html
http://scienceworld.wolfram.com/biography/Lavoisier.html
http://www.chemheritage.org/EducationalServices/chemach/fore/all.html
http://mattson.creighton.edu/History_Gas_Chemistry/Lavoisier.html

Information on the French Revolution:
http://chnm.gmu.edu/revolution/
http://userwww.port.ac.uk/andressd/frlinks.htm

Index

48